Art Smart

How to Have Fun with Paper

Stewart Cowley

Please visit our web site at: **www.garethstevens.com**
For a free color catalog describing Gareth Stevens' list
of high-quality books and multimedia programs, call
1-800-542-2595 (USA) or 1-800-461-9120 (Canada).
Gareth Stevens Publishing's Fax: (414) 332-3567.

Library of Congress Cataloging-in-Publication Data

Cowley, Stewart.
    How to have fun with paper / by Stewart Cowley.
        p. cm. -- (Art smart)
    Includes index.
    Summary: Presents a variety of projects with paper, including pop-up
cards, Chinese lanterns, and paper hats.
    ISBN 0-8368-1712-5 (lib. bdg.)
    1. Paper work--Juvenile literature. [1. Handicrafts.] I. Title.
II. Series.
TT870.C7   1997
745.54--dc20   96-43311

First published in North America in 1997 by
Gareth Stevens Publishing, A World Almanac
Education Group Company, 330 West Olive Street,
Suite 100, Milwaukee, WI 53212 USA.
Original © 1996 by Regency House Publishing Limited
(Troddy Books imprint), The Grange, Grange Yard, London,
England, SE1 3AG. Text and illustrations by Stewart Cowley.
Additional end matter © 1997 by Gareth Stevens, Inc.

Printed in the United States of America

3 4 5 6 7 8 9 05 04 03 02

Gareth Stevens Publishing
A WORLD ALMANAC EDUCATION GROUP COMPANY

Getting Started

Paper is easy to cut and fold. It can be transformed into various shapes and held in place with glue, staples, or tape. Paper is also easy to decorate. You can draw or paint on it or glue things onto it. Paper comes in many types and colors, and it can be found almost anywhere. Paper is always available to create a work of art!

Some of the types of paper that you can use for the projects in this book include:

- plain white paper
- newspaper
- magazine paper
- construction paper
- thin cardboard
- crepe paper
- wallpaper

Other basic things you will need:

- glue
- tape
- ruler
- stapler and staples
- scissors (the safety kind with round tips)
- pencils, pens, and paints
- needle and thread

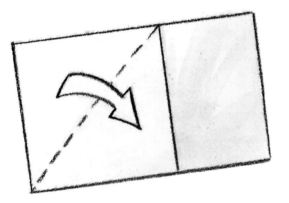

Helpful Hints

Before starting a project: Read the instructions all the way through, and collect all the items you will need.

Cover the surface of your work area with newspaper to make sure you don't scratch it or get glue or paint on it.

And always clean up when you have finished!

To make a perfect square: Fold one corner of a piece of paper diagonally (see dotted line in illustration above) and crease. With scissors, cut off the extra paper along the solid line.

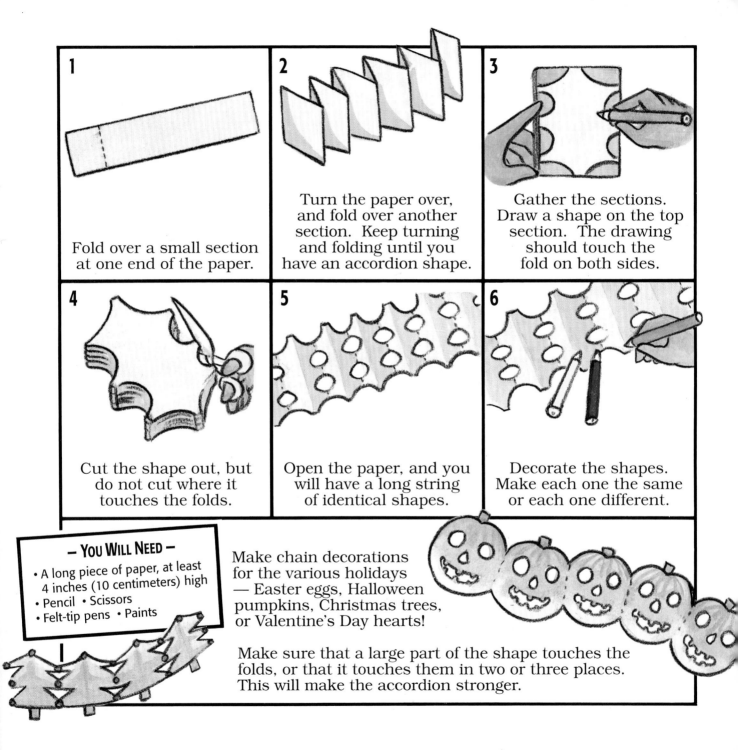

1

Fold over a small section at one end of the paper.

2

Turn the paper over, and fold over another section. Keep turning and folding until you have an accordion shape.

3

Gather the sections. Draw a shape on the top section. The drawing should touch the fold on both sides.

4

Cut the shape out, but do not cut where it touches the folds.

5

Open the paper, and you will have a long string of identical shapes.

6

Decorate the shapes. Make each one the same or each one different.

— YOU WILL NEED —
- A long piece of paper, at least 4 inches (10 centimeters) high
- Pencil • Scissors
- Felt-tip pens • Paints

Make chain decorations for the various holidays — Easter eggs, Halloween pumpkins, Christmas trees, or Valentine's Day hearts!

Make sure that a large part of the shape touches the folds, or that it touches them in two or three places. This will make the accordion stronger.

Chain decorations

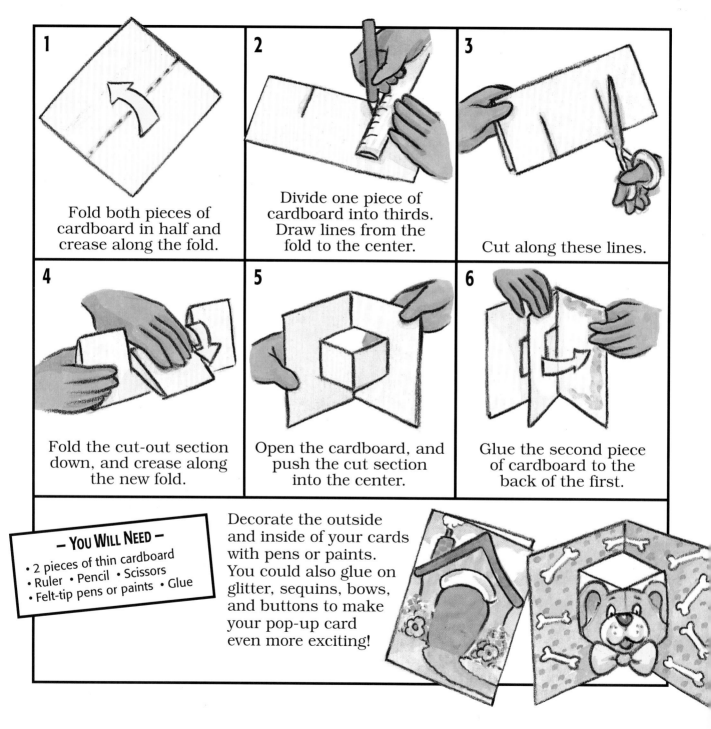

1 Fold both pieces of cardboard in half and crease along the fold.

2 Divide one piece of cardboard into thirds. Draw lines from the fold to the center.

3 Cut along these lines.

4 Fold the cut-out section down, and crease along the new fold.

5 Open the cardboard, and push the cut section into the center.

6 Glue the second piece of cardboard to the back of the first.

— YOU WILL NEED —
• 2 pieces of thin cardboard
• Ruler • Pencil • Scissors
• Felt-tip pens or paints • Glue

Decorate the outside and inside of your cards with pens or paints. You could also glue on glitter, sequins, bows, and buttons to make your pop-up card even more exciting!

Pop-up card

1 Cut a pattern along the top of the rectangular paper, and along the bottom, too, if you like.

2 Draw a line 2 inches (5 cm) from both edges. Draw lines from top to bottom 1 inch (2.5 cm) apart, as shown.

3 Fold the paper in half. Make cuts upward from the fold as far as the 2-inch (5-cm) line.

4 Unfold the paper. Roll it into a tube, and glue the edges together.

5 To make a handle, glue the ends of the strip of cardboard inside the top edge of the lantern.

6 Push down gently so that the sides bulge outward into a lantern shape.

– YOU WILL NEED –
- Rectangle of construction paper 12 inches (30 centimeters) high
- Strip of thin cardboard 1 inch (2.5 cm) wide and 8 inches (20 cm) long
- Crepe paper • Ruler • Glue
- Scissors • Pens or paints
- Pencil • String • Pole

To decorate your lantern, glue crepe paper around the inside of the bottom edge.

Make several lanterns in various sizes and styles. Tie a loop of string on each handle.

Thread a pole through the loops, and hang the lanterns on a patio or porch.

8

Chinese lantern

1 Trim the pictures. Label them 1, 2, and 3.

2 Cut thin cardboard to the same height and total length of all three pictures.

3 Mark the cardboard into 1/2-inch (1-cm) sections. Number the sections and fold the cardboard along the lines, as shown.

4 Mark each picture into 1/2-inch (1-cm) sections. Cut each picture into strips.

5 Glue the strips from picture 1 (in order) onto the sections marked 1.

6 Glue the strips from pictures 2 and 3 (in order) in the same way. Stand the cardboard up and you will see a different picture from the left, the front, and the right.

— YOU WILL NEED —
• Three pictures from an old magazine, trimmed to the same height and width
• A piece of thin cardboard
• Scissors • Pencil
• Ruler • Glue

10

Three-way picture

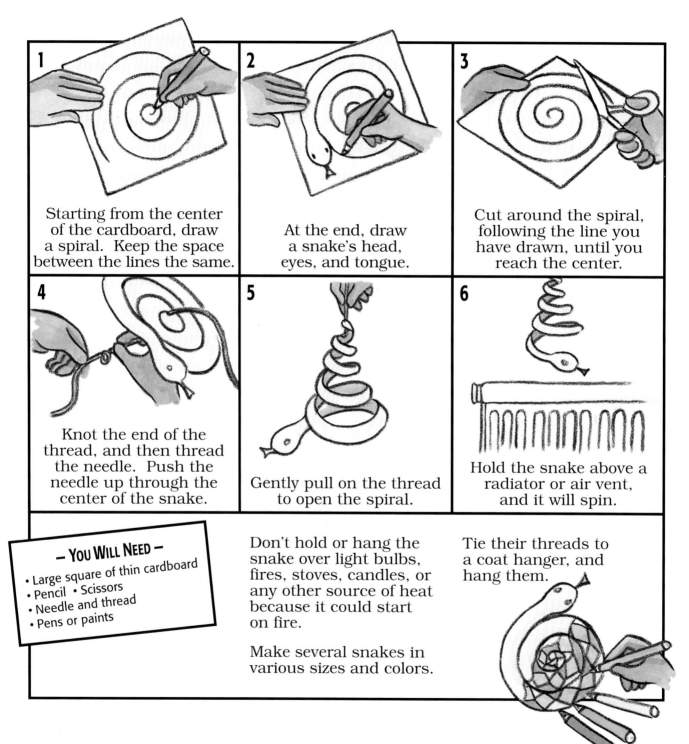

1 Starting from the center of the cardboard, draw a spiral. Keep the space between the lines the same.

2 At the end, draw a snake's head, eyes, and tongue.

3 Cut around the spiral, following the line you have drawn, until you reach the center.

4 Knot the end of the thread, and then thread the needle. Push the needle up through the center of the snake.

5 Gently pull on the thread to open the spiral.

6 Hold the snake above a radiator or air vent, and it will spin.

— YOU WILL NEED —
• Large square of thin cardboard
• Pencil • Scissors
• Needle and thread
• Pens or paints

Don't hold or hang the snake over light bulbs, fires, stoves, candles, or any other source of heat because it could start on fire.

Make several snakes in various sizes and colors.

Tie their threads to a coat hanger, and hang them.

Spinning snake

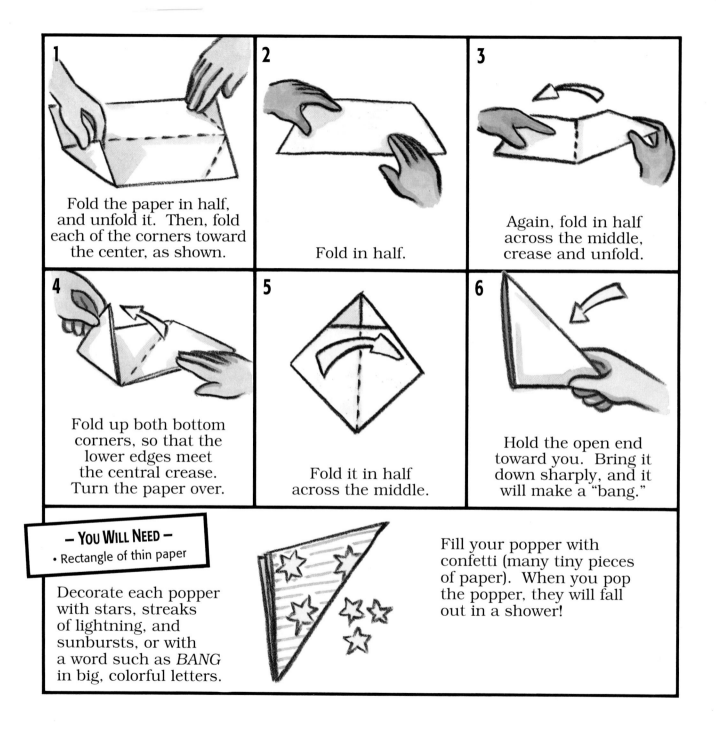

1
Fold the paper in half, and unfold it. Then, fold each of the corners toward the center, as shown.

2
Fold in half.

3
Again, fold in half across the middle, crease and unfold.

4
Fold up both bottom corners, so that the lower edges meet the central crease. Turn the paper over.

5
Fold it in half across the middle.

6
Hold the open end toward you. Bring it down sharply, and it will make a "bang."

— YOU WILL NEED —
• Rectangle of thin paper

Decorate each popper with stars, streaks of lightning, and sunbursts, or with a word such as *BANG* in big, colorful letters.

Fill your popper with confetti (many tiny pieces of paper). When you pop the popper, they will fall out in a shower!

Party popper

1 Fold the paper in half, as shown. Crease along the fold, then unfold it.

2 Fold the top corners toward the crease.

3 Again, fold the top corners toward the crease.

4 Then, fold the paper in half along the middle crease.

5 Fold one side down to the bottom edge. Turn the plane over and do the same on the other side. These are the wings.

6 Flatten out the wings. Hold the portion underneath and launch the airplane!

— YOU WILL NEED —
- A sheet of paper
- Colored pencils or felt-tip pens

Draw a cockpit and wing markings on your airplane.

To launch the airplane, hold it in front of your shoulder, and throw it gently forward and upward. If you launch it too hard, it will nose dive!

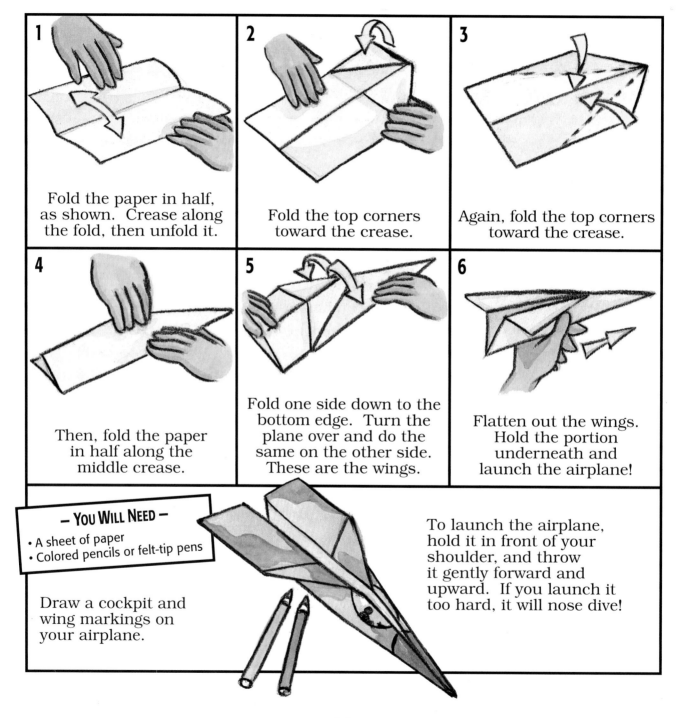

Paper airplane

1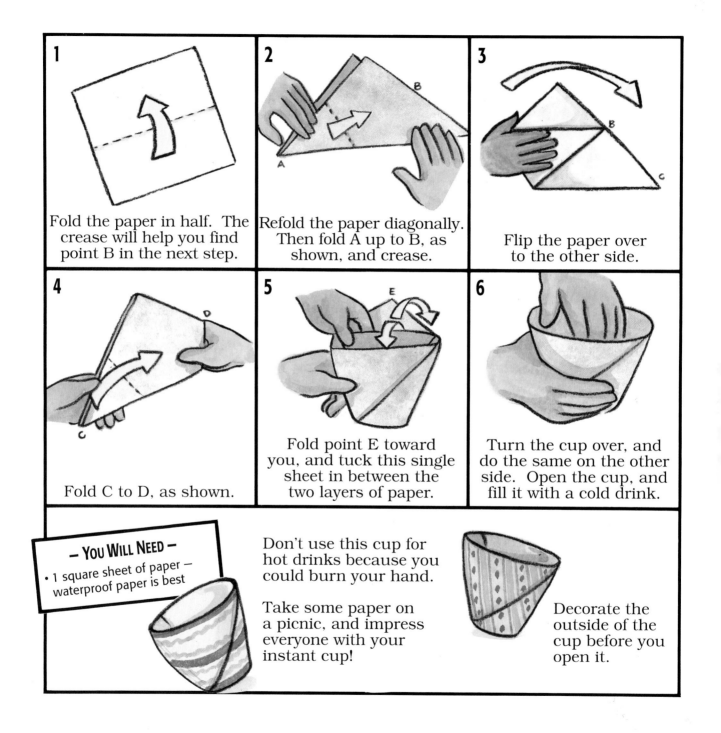
Fold the paper in half. The crease will help you find point B in the next step.

2
Refold the paper diagonally. Then fold A up to B, as shown, and crease.

3
Flip the paper over to the other side.

4
Fold C to D, as shown.

5
Fold point E toward you, and tuck this single sheet in between the two layers of paper.

6
Turn the cup over, and do the same on the other side. Open the cup, and fill it with a cold drink.

— YOU WILL NEED —
• 1 square sheet of paper — waterproof paper is best

Don't use this cup for hot drinks because you could burn your hand.

Take some paper on a picnic, and impress everyone with your instant cup!

Decorate the outside of the cup before you open it.

Paper cup

19

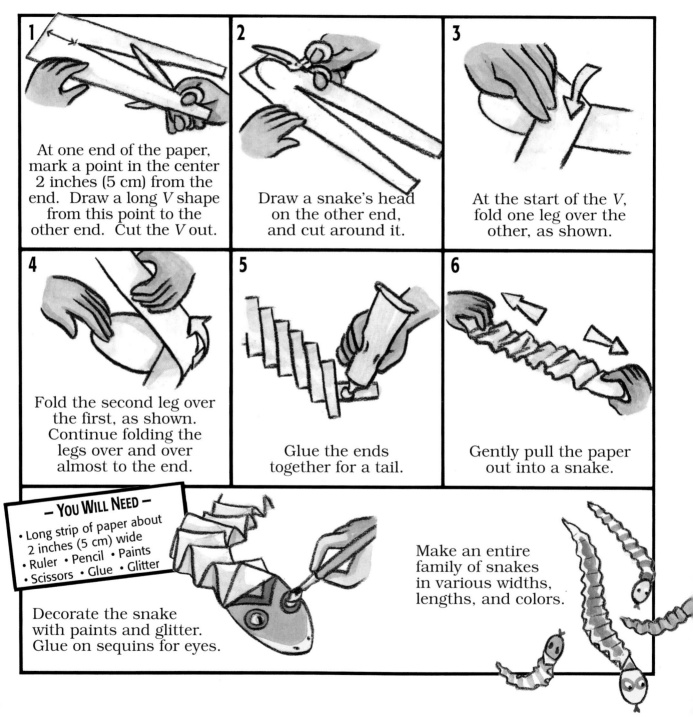

1 At one end of the paper, mark a point in the center 2 inches (5 cm) from the end. Draw a long *V* shape from this point to the other end. Cut the *V* out.

2 Draw a snake's head on the other end, and cut around it.

3 At the start of the *V*, fold one leg over the other, as shown.

4 Fold the second leg over the first, as shown. Continue folding the legs over and over almost to the end.

5 Glue the ends together for a tail.

6 Gently pull the paper out into a snake.

— YOU WILL NEED —
• Long strip of paper about 2 inches (5 cm) wide
• Ruler • Pencil • Paints
• Scissors • Glue • Glitter

Decorate the snake with paints and glitter. Glue on sequins for eyes.

Make an entire family of snakes in various widths, lengths, and colors.

Slippery serpent

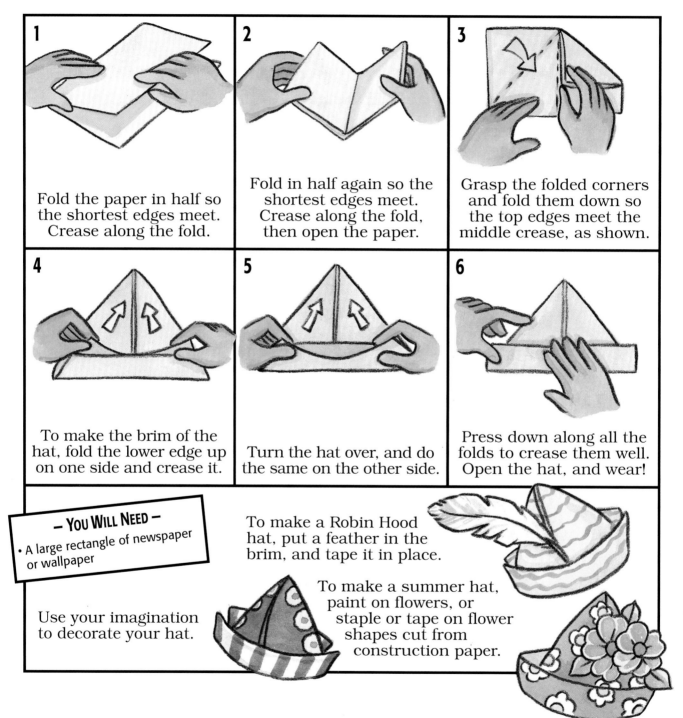

1 Fold the paper in half so the shortest edges meet. Crease along the fold.

2 Fold in half again so the shortest edges meet. Crease along the fold, then open the paper.

3 Grasp the folded corners and fold them down so the top edges meet the middle crease, as shown.

4 To make the brim of the hat, fold the lower edge up on one side and crease it.

5 Turn the hat over, and do the same on the other side.

6 Press down along all the folds to crease them well. Open the hat, and wear!

– YOU WILL NEED –
• A large rectangle of newspaper or wallpaper

To make a Robin Hood hat, put a feather in the brim, and tape it in place.

To make a summer hat, paint on flowers, or staple or tape on flower shapes cut from construction paper.

Use your imagination to decorate your hat.

Paper hat

More Books to Read

Cardboard Carpentry. Janet D'Amato (Lion Books)
Draw, Model, and Paint (series). (Gareth Stevens)
Fun with Paper. Heather Amery (Random)
Paper Capers. Imogene Forte (Incentive Publications)
The Paper Hat Book. Andrew Bennett (Running Press)
Papercrafts. Judith H. Corwin (Watts)
Play with Paper. Sara Lynn and Diane James (Lerner Group)
Worldwide Crafts (series). (Gareth Stevens)

Videos

Art Magic. (Touchstone Art Magic)
Collage Methods. (Crystal Productions)
Paper Construction. (AIMS Media)
Paper Play. (Morris Video)
Paper Sculpture Animals. (Agency for Instructional Technology)

Web Sites

http://www.go-interface.com/fridgeartz
http://finalfront.com/kids/art/art.htm

Index